HOPE

Krishna Yoganarasimha

ISBN 978-93-5559-158-6
© Krishna Yoganarasimha 2021
Published in India 2021 by Pencil

Contributors:
Illustrator: Krishna Yoganarasimha

A brand of
One Point Six Technologies Pvt. Ltd.
123, Building J2, Shram Seva Premises,
Wadala Truck Terminal, Wadala (E)
Mumbai 400037, Maharashtra, INDIA
E connect@thepencilapp.com
W www.thepencilapp.com

DISCLAIMER: *The opinions expressed in this book are those of the authors and do not purport to reflect the views of the Publisher.*

Author biography

Krishna Yoganarasimha was once in the clutches of a global monster called corporate. Even with education he could not save himself. After 15 years of struggle and exploring self in the vast valleys of his mind, he found his true form, his ikigai. He now writes for young minds to help them discover themselves early in life so not to lose a lot of precious time.

CONTENTS

I

Awhite stratus cloud drifts along the azure sky as the mild winds push it further away. In the garden, Nidhi's mother takes care of the blooming flowers. The garden looks like a perfectly choreographed ballet of aromatic flowers. It is the start of spring, and the schools have closed. 10-year-old Nidhi sits at the edge of the garden leaning against the wall. She watches her mother from a distance while playing with her favorite doll. Occasionally she looks at the clouds moving away from her and new clouds replacing the old in the blue sky. It was all dramatic for Nidhi. She had never witnessed the clouds behaving like this before. Nonetheless, the comforting breeze kissed her face, and she smiled and continued playing. Nidhi is a kind-hearted and thoughtful girl. She cares for her toys customarily and mostly spends her time alone. A soft-spoken, spirited, and adorable Nidhi is the darling of all the villagers. As she draped the toy and combed its hair, a thought arose in her. She closes her eyes and remembers this memorable moment that she had treasured.

A few months ago, during a recess break in school, Nidhi sat alone in the play area with her doll. She played with it by swaying it from left to right in a playful motion. But, the dress got stuck to a nail poking out at the edge of the bench.

And then, PARRR!

Oh! No. Nidhi cried. The dress of the doll tore. Nidhi buries her face in disappointment, holding the toy in her hand. From the corridor of the school campus, Suchi, her teacher, walks clutching a handful of books and approaches Nidhi. Nidhi, what happened? Why are you crying? Nidhi looks up at her teacher Suchi. She runs and hugs her, crying. Suchi holds her in her arms and consoles her. Noticing the torn dress, she kisses Nidhi on the head and walks Nidhi back to the staff room. Nidhi sits in front of Suchi and gapes disenchanted while Suchi sews the torn dress.

Looking at her, still concerned, Suchi tries to talk to her. Nidhi, which flower do you like the most? Suchi asks softly. I like roses, teacher; the red ones. They are so beautiful, exquisite, and eye-catching. Aren't they? Nidhi wipes her tears. Oh yes, they are. I like roses too. Suchi looks at her while she continues to hem. A few moments later, Suchi hands over the doll to Nidhi. Nidhi looks at the dress and notices a red rose on the skirt. Nidhi is ecstatic and says, wow! a red rose.

Thank you so much, teacher. The rose looks so lovely. I will go and show it to my friends and my mother. Nidhi runs in the corridor while Suchi looks at her enamored.

Back at the garden, Nidhi opens her eyes. She smiles gently and glances up at the terrace of the neighbor's house. Some boys from the village are readying to fly their kites. Nidhi stands up and runs to her mother. Maa! Maa! The boys are prepping to fly kites. Please, can I also go up to our terrace and watch? Her mother nods but warns her. Be careful and keep an eye on the edges. Stay within the perimeter drawn by your father. Yes, maa. Nidhi shouts as she runs up on the spiral stairs inside the house and opens the door with all her energy.

CREEEEAK! the door opens.

The terrace did not have a retaining wall, but it had a beautiful view of the entire village and the paddy fields that surrounded it. Nidhi walks up slowly to the square mark drawn by her father and stands within it. She watches the boys release their kites one by one. As the kites reach the skies, Nidhi stares at them as they cruise with the wind up in the sky. There were so many kites up there. Nidhi looks to her left and spots the corner where she can see the street and her father's shop. Her father owns a cosmetic shop in the village. She waves her hand at her father, and he waves back. Nidhi smiles.

Up in the sky, a battle of kites is in play. The boys struggle hard to cut the strings of other kites to win the game. The winds take the kites higher and higher. Moments later, a yellow kite and red kite tangle up, the boys shout and pull the strings to cut one another's flight. Suddenly, the yellow kite stops flapping and turns in the opposite direction. It pops up. And, in a blur, the yellow kite tumbles down towards the ground. The boys laugh and squeal. Red wins! Red wins! The yellow kite glides over a building and lands in her aunt's garden nearby. The garden looked big, and roses had bloomed. Nidhi's aunt sold roses that she grew in the village market.

Nidhi watches the yellow kite crash into her aunt's garden, and she spots the roses in full bloom. The roses reminded her of the dress which her teacher had darned. Ah! My favorite roses. They look so beautiful! Nidhi exhales. Before the spring break, from the day Suchi had seamed a rose on her doll's dress, Nidhi diligently plucked a red rose every day from her aunt's garden and took it to school. She waited until her favorite teacher arrived and gave it to her. It had become a routine for Nidhi and a habit for Suchi to receive them. In return, Suchi smiled and hugged Nidhi every time she received a rose. Nidhi loved the comfort and warmth whenever Suchi hugged her.

One of these days, her teacher Suchi said, Oh! Nidhi, thank you for the roses you have been giving me. These are so beautiful. I love the color of it. Suchi inhales the scent of the roses as she expresses her love for them. Thank you so much, teacher! Even I love roses. My aunt has a huge garden where she grows them. She also lets me pick a rose every day. Nidhi smiles and holds Suchi's hand as they walk. Suchi bends down at Nidhi and looks into her eyes. Nidhi! That is wonderful; your aunt has spent her time nurturing the rose plants by giving them manure and water, providing them plenty of energy. And when the time comes, the plants bestow their love to your aunt by giving her these beautiful red roses. Every day she shares the love of the rose plant with you. So, why don't you grow a rose plant at home? And then, when it starts flowering, you can give me the rose from your plant. Nidhi looks at her teacher with a smile and says, Yes! Maam, one day I will grow these roses, too.

It was such a lovely moment that Nidhi had shared with her teacher. Recalling the event brings a smile to her face. With this thought in mind, Nidhi runs down to her mother. Maa! Maaaa! Why is there no rose plant in our garden? Nidhi asks as she gasps and breathes heavily. We had Nidhi. There were many rose plants when you were a small child years ago. For the last three years, we have not planted it again.

Why is that Maa? Did they stop flowering and spreading love?

HaHa! HaHa! Nidhi's mother bursts into laughter. No, my child. Your father had got new plants and flowers and to manage space we had to replace the rose plants. But, if you want, we can grow them now. But, you will have to take good care of them. Do you want to? Nidhi's mother asks. Yes, Maa! I will take care of them. Nidhi hugs her mother and asks if she can go and meet her father in the store at the corner of the street. Her mother nods but cautions saying, be careful and do not run. Walk along the walls of the building. Do you understand? Yes, mother - Nidhi pushes the gate open and runs to her father. At the store, Nidhi's father is reading the newspaper. He is speaking to a few aged men sitting at the entrance. Noticing Nidhi running into the store, an aged man asks, how are you darling? Why are you not playing today?

Nidhi rushes into the store and says, I am in a hurry! Grandpa. I will speak to you later. The aged men laugh and continue with their ongoing conversation. At the store, Nidhi's father looks at her and asks, what do you want, Nidhi? Without any delay, Nidhi jumps to the point and asks, Papa! I need a red rose plant now. Her father looks at her and says, hmm, Red rose. Okay, I will get you one tomorrow. Nidhi immediately protests and says, no, I need it now. It is urgent, very urgent.

Nidhi's father tries to convince her by saying, Nidhi, it is evening already, and the nursery is closed. I will get you the rose plant tomorrow morning.

Listening to her father, Nidhi starts to cry and protests hard. The aged man sitting outside the shop hears Nidhi's cry and tells her father. Why are you making my darling cry? She is not asking for anything expensive. It is a simple rose plant. Go to my garden, cut a sturdy stem, and plant it immediately. It will grow. Nidhi's father agrees. He folds his newspaper, places it below the counter, and walks to the garden across the street with Nidhi. He cuts a stem, hands it over to Nidhi, and says, here you go. Now stop crying and go home. Give this stem to your mother and ask her to plant it immediately. Nidhi smiles and runs back to her mother with the plant in her hand. In the garden, Nidhi's mother was watering the plants. Maa! Maaa! Wait. Please, plant this rose plant stem right away. Nidhi's mother looks surprised and asks her. Where did you get the plant? Nidhi smiles and says - from grandpa's garden. And, yes, dad helped me. Now, please plant this immediately.

Nidhi's mother takes the stem and plants close to the main door, where Nidhi can nurture it easily. After planting, they wash their hands and walk inside the house. It was dusk already. Nidhi's mother switches on the lights inside the house and steps into the kitchen to cook dinner. A few hours later, Nidhi's father reached home. He asks - did you plant the stem, Nidhi? Comfortably sitting inside her room, Nidhi shouts - Yes! Papa. Maa has asked me to take care of it this summer. So, I will be busy. Her father smiles and acknowledges, Okay! That's like my good girl.

After a while, Nidhi comes out of her room with a book and some crayons in her hand. Papa! Look what I drew today? Taking his eyes off the television, Nidhi's father turns towards her and asks, What magic did you create today, my dear! Nidhi jumps on her father's lap, looks at him with a smile, and says, I drew my rose plant. But what color do I paint the rose? Her father thinks, hmm, why not the color red? You have planted it today.

A few minutes later, Nidhi's mother comes announcing. Okay! Come on now, both of you. Come, have your dinner. Nidhi, keep your books back on the shelf and wash your hands before having dinner.

While having dinner, Nidhi asks, how does the rose plant grow from a stem, Maa?. I have seen you putting saplings and seeds and never a stem. Her mother explains while serving food to Nidhi. Just like some recipes need different masalas to taste differently. Some plants grow differently.

So, in this case, rose plants usually grow faster when we use their stem cutting. Ahh! Okay! Nidhi swallows her food. GULP! Nidhi continues her chatter with her father and narrates what she did all day. She also explained the fate of the yellow kite, which got cut by the red kite. The talk goes on and on even after dinner. A few minutes later, she falls asleep on her father's lap while he watches TV.

In the morning, Nidhi opens her eyes from a deep sleep and screams, My rose!. She had been dreaming about her rose. She picks herself up in a flash and runs out to the garden. Maa! Maa! Nidhi starts calling her mother. Her mother is already awake and is in the garden, nurturing the plants. What is it, my child? Maa! What should I do for the rose plant to grow? Hmm, take some of that manure and place it around the plant. Apply some to the fresh cut on the stem as well. Nidhi's mother looks behind her and points her finger at the cow dung pile. Nidhi asks, why Maa? Her mother looks at her and explains. Cow dung has a lot of nutrients that the rose plant likes. You will also need to give water once a day. The soil supports the plant with more ground nutrients when watered well. They are like food for them to grow. Nidhi says, Oh! Is it just the way you give rice, chapati, and milk for me to grow healthier? Nidhi's mother says, yes, exactly. So, is the plant my child now? Nidhi picks up the cow dung. Yes, if you take good care of it, the plant will share love in return with a beautiful red rose. Nidhi applies the manure to the tip of the stem and spreads some of it at the base. Yes, even mam said the same, then when it flowers, I can share this love with others.

All summer, Nidhi takes good care of the rose plant and observes the plant grow. Slowly, the stem gave birth to fresh leaves. And from new leaves to many more other leaves. As the days passed, the plant grew to a height of almost half of Nidhi's. She had taken good care of the plant by watering it daily and nurturing it as taught by her mother.

II

Days went by, and Nidhi had built a routine for herself to wake up early every day and nurture her rose plant. Her passion for the plant increased every day. Nidhi played with her doll sitting beside the plant. She also did her summer assignments while her plant grew. Her summer vacation was about to end, and the schools announced the reopening dates. Nidhi was excited, but she was worried that her rose plant had not flowered yet. Two days before the start of school, a concerned Nidhi walks up to her mother and asks, Maa! It has been so many days since the plant has not given me a rose yet. I took good care of it all summer. Why has the plant not bestowed me with a rose? Nidhi's mother turns and looks at her. Seeing her daughter concerned and losing hope, she bends down to her and explains. Nidhi, the plant will give you a rose when the right time comes. We should never expect love from anyone. If we are blessed, we will be bestowed with love. Lots of love. Love must be unconditional, whatever the situation might be. One day, you will see the outcomes in surprising ways. Wait for it and have patience.

After hearing what her mother said, Nidhi smiles and turns towards the garden and watches her rose plant. Yes, Maa. I think I understand. I will wait for the surprise. Nidhi heads back to her room and gets a pile of books and wrapping paper. She spends her day wrapping her books and labeling them. Nidhi was bored. After a while, she left everything as-is and ran to spend time with her father at the shop. She carried her doll too. That evening, while returning from her father's shop, she happened to glance at the rose plant for one last time for the day. Nidhi notices a tiny bud. It was a rosebud in the rose plant. Ecstatic, Nidhi jumps around with joy and starts calling her mother.

Maa! Maa! Come here, fast.

Her mother runs out and finds Nidhi jumping with joy in the garden. She looks at her and asks, Nidhi, you gave me a shock. What happened? Why are you shouting in the evening? Is everything alright? Nidhi stops jumping. She holds her hand and drags her to the rose plant. Maa! Look, you were right. I am very fortunate and surprised too. The plant has given me the first rosebud. The plant loves me! The plant loves me! Her mother caressing Nidhi's forehead, says Awe! That is so nice, Nidhi. So, by the time your school starts the day after tomorrow, your first rose will be ready. Nidhi interrupts and says - and I will give this rose to my favorite teacher, Suchi mam. Nidhi's mother is happy. She holds Nidhi's hand and walks her inside the house. Come, let the bud grow into a rose. It is getting dark, and it is sleeping time for you and your plant.

A day later, as the sun rose bright and shining. The skies were clear, and Nidhi's first-ever rose bloomed. The petals opened up, and the color of the rose looked fantastic. It filled the air around it with abundant energy. Nidhi wakes up, packs her school bag, and gets ready for school. Wearing her bag, Nidhi asks, Maa! Please help me pluck the rose. Nidhi's mother ties her hair and walks towards the rose plant. Come, this is how you pluck any rose, delicately. Nidhi is happy and heads off to school with her father. Sitting at the back of her father's motorcycle, Nidhi keeps the rose close to her, ensuring it does not get damaged. As soon as they reach the school, Nidhi wishes a good day to her father and walks straight towards the staff room to meet her favorite teacher, Suchi. She glances around and notices all the other teachers. But, there was no sign of Suchi mam. She wishes all the teachers and asks - Good morning, teachers. Where is Suchi mam and when will she arrive?

The teachers knew how close Nidhi was to Suchi. They stare at each other. A teacher walks up to her, Nidhi, Suchi mam is unwell. She will not be coming to school for a while now. Oh, what has happened to her? Where can I meet her? I brought her a rose that I grew in our garden.

The teacher, speaking slowly, explains. Nidhi, the doctors say that Suchi mam will take some days to get well. Why don't you meet her when she is back at school. Nidhi was not convinced. But mam, I do not need much time with her. I just want to give her the rose I grew. The teacher turns towards other teachers in the staff room and exchanges a few expressions. She looks at Nidhi. Hmm, let me see what I can do. The teachers did not want to disappoint her, considering Suchi's condition. Immediately, they call Nidhi's parents to school. Meanwhile, the teacher convinces Nidhi to attend her classes until they make arrangements for Nidhi to meet Suchi.

After a while, Nidhi's parents arrive at school. The teachers explain Suchi's condition to her, and all of them decide that Nidhi has to meet her before it is too late. Nidhi's parents take her to the hospital where Suchi is. On the way, Nidhi asks her father, Papa! Where are we going? Her father patiently explains, Nidhi, you wanted to give your first rose to your Suchi mam, right? So, we are taking you there. Nidhi smiles and looks at the rose that she had in her hand since morning. But Papa! Is Suchi mam unwell? What has happened to her? Nidhi's father remains calm and continues talking to Nidhi. Darling, Suchi mam is slightly ill. Just like you were unwell last year. She is resting in the hospital and waiting to see you.

The nurse at the hospital advised Nidhi and her parents to wait in the lounge area while the doctors examined Suchi. A few minutes passed by, and the hall was silent. The nurse walks out of Suchi's room straight towards Nidhi. Nidhi looks at her. The nurse smiles at Nidhi and informs her parents that Suchi is ready for them now. Nidhi's parents look at her and ask her to go ahead and meet her teacher. Nidhi rushes towards the room to meet her teacher.

In the corridor, Nidhi's parents understand all about Suchi's illness. They were well aware that Suchi stayed alone in the village, and there was no one to support her. The nurse informed them that Suchi's friends and fellow teachers from school are taking turns to visit her and help her out. After hearing this, Nidhi's mother asks, Oh! They are all busy with their daily work. It will be difficult for them to dedicate time to Suchi. Can I stay here and take care of her until she has recovered? The nurse expresses happiness and welcomes their suggestion to remain and take good care of Suchi.

Nidhi pushed the curtains aside and saw her teacher lying on the bed. She looked tired and pale. There was not much energy left in her to even get up and sit straight. Nidhi walks close to her teacher and calls her. Mam, look, I have got you something. Suchi opens her eyes slowly and looks at Nidhi. With a painful voice, she stammers yet expresses delight after seeing Nidhi. Nidhi, how good to see you. How are you doing, my child? Did you enjoy your summer break? Nidhi smiles and stretches her hand to give the rose that she had in her hand since morning. Oh, that is such a beautiful rose, Nidhi. Thank you so much. Is your aunt's garden still filled with roses? Mam, I grew this rose. As you suggested, I planted a rose stem during summer break, and this is the first rose it gave me this morning. I got it for you. Nidhi narrates. Aww, that is so lovely, my dear. So, you have been busy growing your rose plant this summer? Suchi asks as she holds Nidhi's hands and smells the rose.

Yes, mam. I finished all my homework too. Nidhi clarifies. Aren't you a lovely child? I am so proud of you. So, how do you feel after growing your rose plant, Nidhi? Suchi continues to admire the rose while she glances at Nidhi. Mam, I was so happy and spent my mornings nurturing the plant, and in the evening, I watered the plant. I applied manure to the plant to help it grow healthier.

Wow, that sounds wonderful. You have become a big girl now. Who taught you this, Nidhi?

My mother helped me every day, mam. She likes her garden, and she explained how the plant grows and how to take care of it. Thank you for the rose, my dear. You made my day. Suchi expresses her feelings. Nidhi asks curiously. Mam, how long are you staying here? When will you come back to school? Suchi tries to laugh, but she is unable to. Haha! Ahh! She gathers herself quickly and looks at Nidhi. Very soon, my dear. The doctors and nurses are taking good care of me. When I return, I will be brighter than today.

She makes some space for Nidhi to sit down. Suddenly, Suchi realizes something that she had believed and continues speaking. Life, at times, we go through situations that give us pain and sorrow. But it is for us to choose and be hopeful and work through the storm. It is a learning experience for all. We all come out stronger after the storm. That is how life teaches lessons with situations like these. Like the way I teach you at school about new things every day.

As we grow up every day, we experience pain, sorrow, happiness, and triumphs. What keeps us humble and down to earth is hope. Hope strengthens your will and gives you immense energy from within to help you walk through any situation. We always need to be hopeful and feed positive thoughts into our minds.

Suchi was in too much pain but tried her best to hide it. While she spoke to Nidhi, Suchi said to herself to be hopeful and to remain positive. Nidhi did not understand much but nodded to what Suchi said. At the entrance, behind the curtain. Nidhi's parents stood silently and listened to what Suchi had to say. They understood and were in tears. Nidhi looks at her parents standing at the door. Papa, Maa! Look, Suchi mam is here. She liked the rose that I grew during summer break. Nidhi's parents walk closer. You are a wonderful girl, my darling. Nidhi's mother looks at Suchi and gives her hope. You will be fine. There is nothing to worry about, mam. From today, I will be here for you until you recover. We have already spoken to the nurse. Suchi tries to hide her tears. Oh, that was not necessary. The nurses take good care of me. Nidhi jumps into the conversation. Oh! Teacher, do not worry! My mother cooks well. I love it when she cooks rajma and rice. Nidhi looks at her mother and asks, Maa! Will you prepare rajma and rice today? Everyone in the room bursts into laughter after hearing Nidhi.

Haha! Haha! Hehe! Suchi joins too.

Nidhi's mother sits beside Suchi and holds her hand. There is nothing to worry about, for you are not a burden on us. We love meeting you. It is our pleasure to be helpful to someone in need. Nidhi's mother stands up and looks at Nidhi. Nidhi, come, you have to get back to school. And your mam needs to rest. Now, say goodbye to your teacher. Nidhi hugs her teacher and says - Mam, I will get you a rose every Monday morning. Suchi smiles. Yes! Make sure it is from your plant itself. Nidhi's parents wish for her faster recovery, and they all leave. After meeting Nidhi and her parents, a ray of hope glistened on Suchi's face. She turns towards the window and looks at the sun, beaming through the curtains. She closes her eyes and baths in sunlight, hoping to recover soon.

During summer, while Nidhi spent time playing and nurturing her plant, Suchi is made aware of the gruesome fact that she is living in the early stages of bone cancer. Suchi was in a lot of pain as her bones started to weaken. Suchi lived alone after she lost her parents a few years ago. She was young and loved teaching. Moving away from the city, she settled in the village and worked as a teacher in the school. She had no intention of marrying, as teaching kids gave her peace and fulfillment. Post-school, she usually spent time reading books and stayed late in the library reading books of all genres. During classes, she spent a lot of time telling stories to children, and she was amongst one of the favorite teachers at school. Suchi stayed simple and did not indulge in looking beautiful as there was no need for it. She was pretty by nature and kept her hair short.

For the next seven months, Nidhi's parents took good care of Suchi at the hospital and later at her house. And every Monday, Nidhi got a fresh red rose for her favorite teacher. Suchi responded well to the love and care showered on her by her friends, colleagues, and especially Nidhi's parents. Suchi started to show signs of recovery. The doctors were hopeful about her recovery.

A few days later, it was like a new star in the night sky emerging from the darkness and shining bright. Suchi had recovered and was back on her feet. She had dealt with the pain for eight long months, and it was all good now. She slowly started to do her chores, and the doctors signed off on her after regular monitoring. She returned to school, and a heroic welcome awaited her for fighting boldly with cancer and not losing hope. During the assembly, Suchi walks up to the podium and looks around. The teachers and students look at Suchi with a gentle smile.

Hope is a good thing. Sometimes a little support, an innocent gesture, and a helping hand can flip lives for good. The impact on the person is massive. Eight months ago, I had given up. There was no hope left in me. Even when the doctors said I would be fine, I had quit already. Today, I am standing in front of you, filled with gratitude only because of hope. I want to thank all of you for supporting me and taking care of me. But, I want to convey a special thanks to a person who revived hope in me in the most innocent way possible. Suchi looks at Nidhi, sitting amongst other students. This person shared love and gave me a reason to strengthen the dying hope in me. It was a red rose. I waited for it every Monday and hoped to see it again, every other Monday. The person never failed to deliver. Thank you for reinstating hope in me. I dedicate the below lines to this person, and they have a special place in my life forever.

There I was, on the dying table,

Trying hard, but was unable,

I counted days and looked hopeless,

Fighting with self to readily express!

Then, you walked in with a red rose,

That gave me hope, and to compose,

I owe you for your simplicity and grace,

Unknowingly helping me overcome and ace!

Notes

What did you learn from this story?